Spelling P.A.C.T.

Parents and Children Together

by

Lynne Ecenbarger

AuthorHouse™
1663 Liberty Drive, Suite 200
Bloomington, IN 47403
www.authorhouse.com
Phone: 1-800-839-8640

AuthorHouse™ UK Ltd.
500 Avebury Boulevard
Central Milton Keynes, MK9 2BE
www.authorhouse.co.uk
Phone: 08001974150

First published by AuthorHouse 5/24/2006

ISBN: 1-4208-4967-0 (sc)

Library of Congress Control Number: 2005904557

Printed in the United States of America
Bloomington, Indiana

This book is printed on acid-free paper.

Bloomington, IN Milton Keynes, UK

authorHOUSE

Dedication

This book is dedicated to my husband,
Steve, my angel on earth.

Rainbow Spelling

Have your child write her words using large letters. Then she can trace over them three times each with a different colored crayon for rainbow spelling!

"On the Back" Spelling

Have your child "write" a spelling word with her pointer finger on your back. Try to guess which spelling word she wrote. Now you write one on your child's back while she tries to guess which one it is.

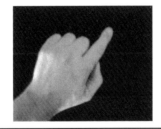

Configuration Games

Help your child write her spelling words on paper and ask her to draw the outline of each word. Then have her cut out the words along the outlines. Cover up the letters and have her try to guess each word based on its configuration.

example grab *example*

Parents,

Please spend five to ten minutes each day with your child helping him / her study their words and initial below beside each day. Then please return this sheet on Friday with your child. Thank you!

Monday _____   Wednesday _____
Tuesday _____   Thursday _____

A Hunting We Will Go

Have your child look for her spelling words in magazines, newspapers, and catalogs. Allow her to cut out each word and paste it on a piece of paper.

Right or Wrong

Write three of your child's spelling words on a piece of paper, with one being misspelled. Your child decides which one is incorrect and spells it correctly. Continue until all spelling words have been spelled by your child.

Exercise Spelling

Have your child touch her toes while she spells all her one-syllable words. Have her do jumping jacks while she spells her two-syllable words.

Parents,

Please spend five to ten minutes each day with your child helping him / her study their words and initial below beside each day. Then please return this sheet on Friday with your child. Thank you!

Monday _____   Wednesday _____
Tuesday _____   Thursday _____

Invisible Spelling

Have your child write her words using a small paintbrush and water. She can brush the water onto a countertop, refrigerator door, etc. As it evaporates, your appliance is clean!

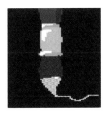

Cereal Spelling

Let your child spell her words using alphabet cereal.

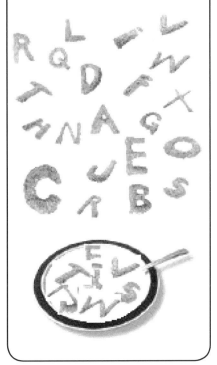

Ten Questions

Have your child write one of her words on a card. Then ask questions of your child that can be answered by a *yes* or a *no*. When you think you know the word, announce it and spell it. Then let your child try to guess a spelling word you've written by asking *yes*/*no* questions.

Parents,

Please spend five to ten minutes each day with your child helping him / her study their words and initial below beside each day. Then please return this sheet on Friday with your child. Thank you!

Monday _____   Wednesday _____

Tuesday _____   Thursday _____

Bedtime Spelling

Before retiring for bed, write your child's spelling words on separate pieces of paper. Hide them in different places in your child's bedroom (i.e.; under her pillow, in her medicine cabinet where she keeps her toothbrush, etc). When she finds any of the pieces of paper she must give the paper to you and spell the word correctly that is written on the paper. If she can spell it, she gets to keep the paper. If not, she must let you hide it in another place the next evening. The object is to collect all the words (papers) before the end of the school week.

Macaroni Spelling

Let your child spell the words using macaroni letters.

Glue Rubbings

Assist your child with spelling her words on paper using glue. When the glue dries, she can put another piece of paper down on top of her words and rub lightly with a pencil. The words will appear in shaded form!

Parents,

Please spend five to ten minutes each day with your child helping him / her study their words and initial below beside each day. Then please return this sheet on Friday with your child. Thank you!

| Monday | _____ | Wednesday | _____ |
| Tuesday | _____ | Thursday | _____ |

Cut-up Words

After your child writes each of her words, have her cut them up and allow you to rearrange them back in order.

Pudding Spelling

Have your child trace her spelling words in pudding!

True Test

Have your child dictate her words to you in spelling-test fashion. For instance, she may say, "Number 1 is *drum* - spell *drum*." After you spell, she checks your spelling. She can give you a smile or star if spelled correctly! You may want to misspell one or two on purpose just to give her a chance to edit for misspellings and have her tell you the correct spelling.

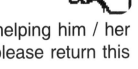

Parents,

Please spend five to ten minutes each day with your child helping him / her study their words and initial below beside each day. Then please return this sheet on Friday with your child. Thank you!

Monday _____   Wednesday _____
Tuesday _____   Thursday _____

All Tangled Up

Take the vowels /a/, /e/, /i/, /o/, /u/, and each of the consonants from this week's words. Write them on individual pieces of paper. Each sheet of paper should be the same size and be large enough to stand on. Place them in random order on the floor in a 5" x 3" grid. As you call out one of the spelling words your child will place hands and/or feet on the appropriate letters to spell it back to you.

Stringing Along Your Spelling Words

Have your child spell her words by forming the letters with pieces of yarn or string.

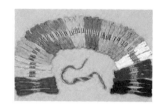

Don't You Laugh!

Begin drawing one of your child's spelling words. The object is for your child to guess which word it is and to write it down (spell it) before you get done drawing it!

Parents,

Please spend five to ten minutes each day with your child helping him / her study their words and initial below beside each day. Then please return this sheet on Friday with your child. Thank you!

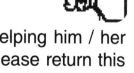

Monday _____   Wednesday _____
Tuesday _____   Thursday   _____

Go Fish

Make a set of spelling word cards by writing each word twice on separate pieces of paper. Recipe cards work well for this game. Include pairs of words from previous lists to reinforce the spelling of these words as well. Deal out five cards to every player. Lay the remaining cards face-down in a stack in the middle. Each player will take out any pairs they have in their hands. Then one player begins by asking another for one of the words they need to make a pair for themselves. If the player asked has the word, she must give it to the one who asked. If they do not have it, the asking player draws from the stack in the middle. If the word is drawn, the player lays it down with her other pairs and asks again for a different word. If not, the player adds the card to her hand and play continues. As all pairs are formed, each player must be able to spell the word on her pairs in order to keep the pair.

Raisin Spelling

Have your child spell her words by forming the letters with raisins.

Parents,

Please spend five to ten minutes each day with your child helping him / her study their words and initial below beside each day. Then please return this sheet on Friday with your child. Thank you!

Monday _____   Wednesday _____
Tuesday _____   Thursday   _____

Shaving Cream Spelling

Have your child write her words in shaving cream!

Tape Recordings

Tape record your child spelling her words out loud. Then let her listen to the tape.

Sponge Spelling

Lay out foam or sponge letters and let your child spell her words by dipping the sponges in paint.

Parents,

Please spend five to ten minutes each day with your child helping him / her study their words and initial below beside each day. Then please return this sheet on Friday with your child. Thank you!

Monday _____   Wednesday _____
Tuesday _____   Thursday _____

Acrostic Spelling

Have your child write her spelling words (on separate pieces of paper) going down the left margin vertically. Ask her to write another word she knows for each of the letters in the individual spelling words.

f rom
o ver
r an

Popcorn Spelling

Pop some popcorn and let your child form her spelling words using the popcorn pieces.

Create Their Own Sentences

Have your child take any three of her spelling words and write out a spelling sentence. Continue until all words are used in sentences.

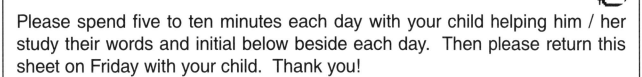

Parents,

Please spend five to ten minutes each day with your child helping him / her study their words and initial below beside each day. Then please return this sheet on Friday with your child. Thank you!

Monday _____   Wednesday _____
Tuesday _____   Thursday   _____

Spelling Words Worth

Assign numerical values to each of the letters. For example:

/a/ = 1 /b/ = 2
/c/ = 3 /d/ = 4

and so on. As your child writes her words, she can "add up" how much each one is worth to see which one has the most numerical value.

Making the Fit

Start by telling your child she will use one of her spelling words to complete your sentence. Then she will write the appropriate word on her paper. Some sentences you might give orally would be, "Those flowers had the shortest (say "blank" here) I've ever seen." Ask her to tell you which one

of her spelling words would "fit" in the blank. Then ask her to write just the word (not the sentence).

Cotton Ball Spelling

Have your child spell out her words by gluing cotton balls down on the paper to form the letters.

Parents,

Please spend five to ten minutes each day with your child helping him / her study their words and initial below beside each day. Then please return this sheet on Friday with your child. Thank you!

Monday _____   Wednesday _____
Tuesday _____   Thursday   _____

Starts the Same

Cut pictures out of magazines and lay them as headers on top of a table or desk. Have your child spell her words under the correct column where the picture starts with the same beginning sound.

because   under   laugh

Simon Says

Play the traditional game of *Simon Says* by having your child spell the words correctly when you say the magical words. This game could continue on into the evening up to bedtime. Your child could also take turns being "Simon".

Word Clues

Give your child specific clues to spell each of her words. For instance, the first clue could be, "It's your spelling word that is a contraction." If she cannot guess the word based on this clue, give her another such as, "It begins with /c/."

Parents,

Please spend five to ten minutes each day with your child helping him / her study their words and initial below beside each day. Then please return this sheet on Friday with your child. Thank you!

Monday _____   Wednesday _____
Tuesday _____   Thursday _____

Hopping on One Foot

Ask your child to hop on her left foot while spelling her first spelling word, her right foot while spelling her second spelling word, etc. If she misspells a word she can hop on both feet to spell it again.

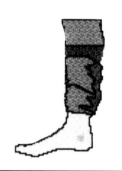

Type It

Allow your child to type out her words on a computer keyboard or typewriter. If there is not one in the home, make a simulated keyboard out of cardboard or heavy paper and cover with contact paper. She will use her fingers to "spell" out her words but will have no hard copy of her lists printed.

Picture Spelling

Find pictures of all your child's spelling words in catalogs or magazines. Put them in a shoe box. Take turns drawing from the box and spelling the word that represents the picture.

Parents,

Please spend five to ten minutes each day with your child helping him / her study their words and initial below beside each day. Then please return this sheet on Friday with your child. Thank you!

Monday _____   Wednesday _____
Tuesday _____   Thursday _____

Grocery Bag Vests

Make a vest from a grocery bag by laying it flat and cutting two arm-holes and a neck-hole. Have your child's spelling words written on pieces of paper. Quiz her on the spelling of her words one at a time. If she can spell her word, she gets to keep the paper, illustrate the word, and then paste it on her vest.

It might take a couple evenings before she can complete her vest.

Blink and Wink

Ask your child to wink with her left eye while spelling her first spelling word. She then winks with her right eye while spelling her second word. If she misspells any words she should blink with both eyes while spelling the word again.

Fill in the Blank

Write out your child's spelling words, leaving blank spaces in some. Then ask your child to write the missing letters in the appropriate spaces.

Parents,

Please spend five to ten minutes each day with your child helping him / her study their words and initial below beside each day. Then please return this sheet on Friday with your child. Thank you!

Monday _____   Wednesday _____
Tuesday _____   Thursday _____

Sorting

Ask your child to write each of the words for the week on individual strips of paper. Begin by taking two words that have something in common and asking your child why you sorted these two together. For instance, you could pull out the words "fuss" and "Russ" and your child could tell you they are alike because they both have /uss/ in them. Other ways to sort are for number of letters, beginning sounds, ending sounds, number of vowels, etc.

Please Sit Down

Tape your child's spelling words to the bottom of the chairs where you sit to eat dinner and breakfast. Before sitting down to eat, have your child look under her seat and ask you how to spell the word that is taped there. If you can spell it, you can sit in her seat for that meal. Then you ask her to spell the word that is under a different seat to see which chair she gets to sit in.

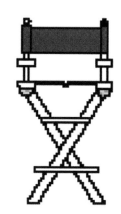

Parents,

Please spend five to ten minutes each day with your child helping him / her study their words and initial below beside each day. Then please return this sheet on Friday with your child. Thank you!

Monday _____   Wednesday _____
Tuesday _____   Thursday _____

Cheerleader Spelling

This involves your child moving her arms to one of three positions according to how "tall" the letter is when we print it. All tall letters (h, k, l, etc.) would be demonstrated by putting both arms straight up to the air with elbows locked. Medium height letters (a, n, s, etc.) would have elbows bent with tips of fingers or fists touching the shoulders. Letters that drop below the line (g, p, j, etc.) would show arms extending straight down to the side. As you call out a spelling word, your child will "cheerleader spell" it with her arms and cheerleader voices.

Sticky Note Spelling

Write each of your child's spelling words in a line on a piece of paper. Cover all but the first letter of each word with a sticky note. Ask your child to spell each word, one at a time, as you pull the note off, slowly revealing the correct spelling.

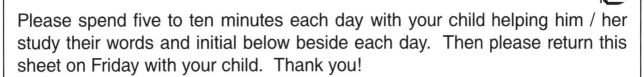

Parents,

Please spend five to ten minutes each day with your child helping him / her study their words and initial below beside each day. Then please return this sheet on Friday with your child. Thank you!

Monday _____   Wednesday _____
Tuesday _____   Thursday _____

Flashlight Spelling

Have your child write her words by shining a flashlight against a wall in the house.

Sandpaper Spelling

Have a supply of letters cut from sandpaper. Allow your child to spell her words using these sandpaper letters.

Rhyming Pictures

Cut pictures from magazines that rhyme with this week's words and lay them as headers on the table or desk. Have your child spell her words under the correct column where the picture rhymes with the word.

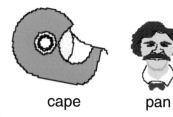

cape   pan

Parents,

Please spend five to ten minutes each day with your child helping him / her study their words and initial below beside each day. Then please return this sheet on Friday with your child. Thank you!

Monday _____   Wednesday _____

Tuesday _____   Thursday   _____

Slow Drip Spelling

Dip a straw into a glass of water and, holding your finger over the top of the straw to close off the air, lift the straw out of the glass. Show your child how to spell her words by using water from the straw as you slowly remove your finger from the top of the straw.

Ball Toss Spelling

Toss a small ball to your child and begin spelling one of her spelling words. She should toss it back to you and add the next letter. Continue in this fashion until each word is spelled.

Playing Cards

Take out the face cards to a deck of playing cards. Lay the rest face down in the center of the players. Ask your child to spell a word and then have her draw a card. If she spells the word correctly she gets the number of points that shows on the card. Take turns until all words are spelled.

Parents,

Please spend five to ten minutes each day with your child helping him / her study their words and initial below beside each day. Then please return this sheet on Friday with your child. Thank you!

Monday _____   Wednesday _____
Tuesday _____   Thursday _____

Golfing

Tape your child's spelling words individually to the bottom of paper cups. Using a small ball and broom (or golf club and ball, if available) allow your child to stand five feet from the cups and try to putt the ball into each of the cups. If she gets the ball into a cup, ask her to spell the word on the bottom of the cup.

Sidewalk Spelling

Have your child write her words on the sidewalk outside using sidewalk chalk.

Chocolate Chip Spelling

Have your child write her words using tiny chocolate chips to form the letters in each of her words.

Parents,

Please spend five to ten minutes each day with your child helping him / her study their words and initial below beside each day. Then please return this sheet on Friday with your child. Thank you!

Monday _____   Wednesday _____
Tuesday _____   Thursday _____

Blanket-Ball Spelling

Put a blanket in between you and your child on the floor. Place a small ball in the middle of the blanket. As you call out one of this week's spelling words, both you and your child should grasp the blanket by the edges and begin lifting it while shaking gently and spelling the word. Your voices should go up in volume as the blanket rises. Once the word is spelled, start lowering the blanket and spell the same word by lowering your voices so by the time the blanket reaches the ground your voices are in a very low tone. Try not to spill the ball from the blanket.

Parts of Speech

Have your child spell her words by categorizing them according to parts of speech.

nouns	verbs	adjectives

Parents,

Please spend five to ten minutes each day with your child helping him / her study their words and initial below beside each day. Then please return this sheet on Friday with your child. Thank you!

Monday _____   Wednesday _____

Tuesday _____   Thursday _____

Puzzled Spelling

Ask your child to write each of her spelling words separately on a recipe card and to decorate the background of the card. Then take each card and cut it into three or four pieces, jigsaw puzzle fashion. She can put the puzzle pieces together as she spells her words.

Up With Spelling

Have your child volley a ball in the air while spelling each one of her words. Beach balls work well for this activity.

Pretzel Spelling

Have your child spell her words by bending pretzels into the letters to form each word.

Parents,

Please spend five to ten minutes each day with your child helping him / her study their words and initial below beside each day. Then please return this sheet on Friday with your child. Thank you!

Monday _____   Wednesday _____
Tuesday _____   Thursday _____

The Wave

Your child can do the "wave" when spelling her words for this week. She folds her hands together and goes up for the vowels and down for the consonants.

Tap Spell

Have your child tap with a ruler as she spells her words for the week. To make this more interesting, you can start to "tap spell" a word, stop in the middle, and ask your child to continue where you left off.

Spell to Win

Collect a set of letter cards necessary to spell this week's words. Begin by calling out one of the words. Your child must select the appropriate letter cards and arrange them in order to spell the word. She may then give you a word to spell with the letter cards.

Parents,

Please spend five to ten minutes each day with your child helping him / her study their words and initial below beside each day. Then please return this sheet on Friday with your child. Thank you!

Monday _____ Wednesday _____

Tuesday _____ Thursday _____

Wheel of Fortune®

Draw blanks on a piece of paper to represent the letters in one of this week's spelling words. Have your child do the same, but do not tell each other what word you were each thinking of. Your child may begin by asking for a letter. If it is in your word, write it in the appropriate

blank and let her take another turn. If it is not in your word, you take turns asking for letters in her word that she drew blanks for. Play continues until one player gets the entire word spelled.

Word Stairs

Spell this week's words using *word stairs*, where the first letter in the new word is the same as the last letter in the word that preceded it, written in stair-like fashion.

example only

```
o f t e n
        o
        n
        e v e r y
                e
                l
                l
                o
                w
```

example only

Parents,

Please spend five to ten minutes each day with your child helping him / her study their words and initial below beside each day. Then please return this sheet on Friday with your child. Thank you!

Monday _____   Wednesday _____
Tuesday _____   Thursday _____

Concentration

Write each of your child's spelling words twice, once on a colored recipe card and again on a white recipe card. You may want to include numerous pairs of words from previous weeks' spelling lists. Turn them face down in the center between you and your child. Your child begins by taking one colored card and trying to find the matching white one. Once all sets are taken, your child quizes you on the spelling of each set of words. If you can't spell the word, your child gets to steal the set from you, provided she can spell the word! Then quiz your child and try to steal them back!

'Play'ing with Words

Have your child spell her words using playdough.

Jello® Spelling

Sprinkle jello from the box onto a napkin or paper towel. Allow your child to spell each of her words in the jello. Check her spelling after each word. If spelled correctly she gets to lick her finger!

Parents,

Please spend five to ten minutes each day with your child helping him / her study their words and initial below beside each day. Then please return this sheet on Friday with your child. Thank you!

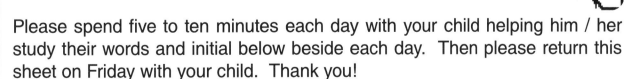

Monday _____   Wednesday _____
Tuesday _____   Thursday   _____

Pipe Cleaner Spelling

Cut a few pipe cleaners into half and quarter lengths. Store them in a resealable plastic bag. Have your child spell the words from her list using the pipe cleaners, bending and turning them into each of the necessary letters to form the word.

Spelling Tag

Allow your child to begin spelling one of her words by saying the first letter. You say the second letter. She says the third, and so on.

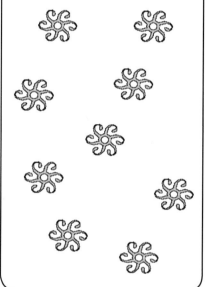

Word Search

Have your child complete a word search puzzle that you construct:

SAMPLE
(not to be used with this week's words)

```
t  w  h  i  s  t  l  e  x
r  e  a  d  y  l  a  v  b
d  h  d  o  c  n  j  s  k
q  p  n  g  r  i  p  h  o
c  j  n  t  e  e  t  h  a
i  i  t  h  g  l  u  s  c
s  h  o  e  s  t  d  f  h
f  o  r  k  s  l  i  t  m
```

Parents,

Please spend five to ten minutes each day with your child helping him / her study their words and initial below beside each day. Then please return this sheet on Friday with your child. Thank you!

Monday _____   Wednesday _____
Tuesday _____   Thursday _____

Rummy Spelling

You will need three sets of letter cards to play this game. Pass out seven letter cards to each player. Lay the rest in the middle and turn the top one face up. One player begins by taking that letter or drawing one from the pile. The object is to be the first to spell two of the spelling words from this week's list.

With each draw, one card is always discarded. Players may lay down a "word" when they have one. They don't have to wait to get both words.

Alphabetical Order

Have your child write her spelling words in ABC order.

Jump Rope Spelling

Allow your child to jump rope while spelling each of her words. You give her a word and she should say a letter for each jump she makes, spelling out the word.

Parents,

Please spend five to ten minutes each day with your child helping him / her study their words and initial below beside each day. Then please return this sheet on Friday with your child. Thank you!

Monday _____   Wednesday _____
Tuesday _____   Thursday _____

"Hide and Go Seek" Spelling

Take the letter cards from last week's *Rummy* game and hide them around the house. Your child must find the letters and spell out her words.

Whipped Cream Spelling

Have your child write her words into whipped cream that has been spooned into a bowl.

Scrabble® Spelling

Have your child use *Scrabble®* game pieces to spell her words. Then have her add the numbers on the tiles to determine the "value" of each word.

Parents,

Please spend five to ten minutes each day with your child helping him / her study their words and initial below beside each day. Then please return this sheet on Friday with your child. Thank you!

Monday _____   Wednesday _____

Tuesday _____   Thursday _____

Felt Letter Spelling

Let your child make her spelling words with letters cut from felt. When cutting the letters make the upper and lower case letters. Also, make the vowels one color and the consonants a different.

Clothesline Spelling

String a bungie cord clothesline between two chairs. Provide numerous clip clothespins with different letters of the alphabet written on them. Your child can clip the correct letters in sequential order on the line to spell her spelling words.

Stamp It

Let your child spell her words by stamping each word with letter stamps and an inkpad.

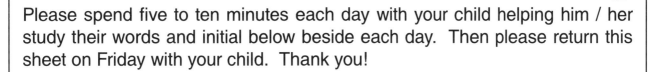

Parents,

Please spend five to ten minutes each day with your child helping him / her study their words and initial below beside each day. Then please return this sheet on Friday with your child. Thank you!

Monday _____   Wednesday _____
Tuesday _____   Thursday _____

Magnetic Letters Spelling

Have your child spell her words using magnetic letters.

Red and Blue Spelling

Have your child write her words by using a red colored pencil, marker, or crayon for all consonants and a blue for all vowels.

Synonyms and Antonyms

Give your child a synonym or antonym for one of her spelling words. She must identify the spelling word and spell it correctly.

Parents,

Please spend five to ten minutes each day with your child helping him / her study their words and initial below beside each day. Then please return this sheet on Friday with your child. Thank you!

Monday _____   Wednesday _____
Tuesday _____   Thursday _____

Roll the Dice

Take turns rolling two dice to see who goes first. The one who rolls the highest number when the two are added together begins. They may choose any spelling word from this week's list to write from memory. If spelled correctly, they get the number of points that their roll totaled. If not, the roll goes to the next person. Continue until all spelling words have been attempted.

Phone Spelling

Using a touchtone phone, write out the corresponding numbers to your child's spelling words for this week, one at a time. Have your child put the correct word beside the appropriate set of numbers.

Scrambled Eggs Spelling

Write each of your child's spelling words in a scrambled fashion. Let your child unscramble each and spell it correctly on a line drawn beside your scrambled version.

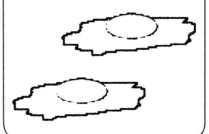

Parents,

Please spend five to ten minutes each day with your child helping him / her study their words and initial below beside each day. Then please return this sheet on Friday with your child. Thank you!

Monday _____   Wednesday _____

Tuesday _____   Thursday _____

Wallpaper Spelling

Cut letters of the alphabet out of textured wallpaper samples. Have your child spell her words using these letters. Then have her trace over the letters with her fingers once the entire word is spelled. Store the letters in a ziplock baggie for future use.

Spelling by the Numbers

Have your child spell, in columns, all the two-letter words, three-letter words, etc.

2-letter words	3-letter words	4-letter words

Checkers Spelling

Write your child's spelling words on small strips of paper and tape them to the bottom of checkers. Now play the game. For every checker of your's that she "jumps", she must be able to spell the word on the bottom. If she can not spell the word, she forfeits the checker to you.

Parents,

Please spend five to ten minutes each day with your child helping him / her study their words and initial below beside each day. Then please return this sheet on Friday with your child. Thank you!

Monday _____   Wednesday _____
Tuesday _____   Thursday _____

Turn - Turn - Turn

Draw two paper circles identical in size and cut them out. Then cut a small rhombus-shaped section out of one of them and attach the two together with a brad in the middle, placing the one with the cut-out section on the top. Write the "word family" on the top circle just to the right of the rhombus cut-out. Write these letters on the blank spaces that you see on the bottom circle as you turn the top circle clockwise:

/b/, /f/, /g/, /n/, /r/, /s/, /sh/, /sp/, /st/

Have your child turn the top circle and read each of the words.

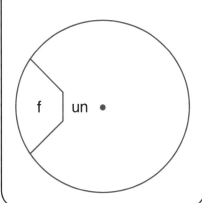

Marshmallow Spelling

Let your child spell her words using miniature marshmallows to form the letters.

Spaghetti Spelling

Cook spaghetti and have your child form the letters to each of her words on her plate before pouring the sauce on top to eat!

Parents,

Please spend five to ten minutes each day with your child helping him / her study their words and initial below beside each day. Then please return this sheet on Friday with your child. Thank you!

Monday _____   Wednesday _____
Tuesday _____   Thursday   _____

Pull and Spell

Write each of your child's spelling words on a piece of paper and cut them into individual letters. Put them into a lunch sack. Have your child draw one letter out and decide whether to keep it or put it back in. The object is for each player to spell a spelling word one at a time, beginning with the first letter.

So once she decides to keep a letter she must complete that word she was working on by spelling it in order and hoping to draw the correct letter in the sequence. Once a word is spelled she can start on a different word.

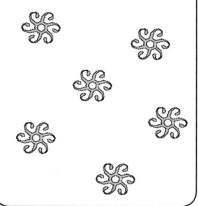

It's Questionable

Choose a word from the spelling list. In order to predict the word, your child must ask questions such as, "Does it have more than one vowel?" Decide in advance how many questions to allow. She writes down her answers. At the end of the game, give the answers.

Parents,

Please spend five to ten minutes each day with your child helping him / her study their words and initial below beside each day. Then please return this sheet on Friday with your child. Thank you!

Monday _____   Wednesday _____
Tuesday _____   Thursday _____

Syllable Spelling

Have your child write her words in columns according to how many syllables there are in each word.

one-syllable words	two-syllable words

In-the-Air Spelling

Have your child extend her arm out in front of her with her thumb up. Ask her to spell her words in the air, forming each of the letters, while focusing on her thumb.

Stencil Spelling

Purchase some inexpensive stencils and have your child "stencil spell" her words.

Parents,

Please spend five to ten minutes each day with your child helping him / her study their words and initial below beside each day. Then please return this sheet on Friday with your child. Thank you!

Monday _____   Wednesday _____
Tuesday _____   Thursday _____

Chocolate Covered Words

Melt chocolate in a pan or in the microwave and have your child spell her words in the cooled, melted chocolate.

Whisper Shout Spelling

Have your child spell her words saying each consonant in her "out-loud" voice and each vowel in a whisper.

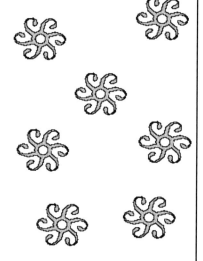

Three-D Spelling Words

Using three different colors of plastic clay or playdough, roll each to pencil thickness. Stack on top of one another and pinch together at the joints. Form the letters to spell this week's words using the colored, layered clay.

Parents,

Please spend five to ten minutes each day with your child helping him / her study their words and initial below beside each day. Then please return this sheet on Friday with your child. Thank you!

Monday _____   Wednesday _____
Tuesday _____   Thursday _____

Cookie Dough Spelling

Help your child form her spelling words using unbaked cookie dough. Then bake the cookies. Ask her to read each one before she can eat it!

Throw it in the Trash

After your child has spelled a spelling word, check it for accuracy. If spelled correctly she gets a chance to wad it up and "shoot" for two points using the garbage can as the "basket". Continue with all words.

Dust the Words

Spray a small amount of lemon dust spray on a piece of wood furniture. Have your child write her words using a dust cloth and her pointer finger on the furniture. Once you've checked for accuracy, allow her to clean the entire piece of furniture.

Parents,

Please spend five to ten minutes each day with your child helping him / her study their words and initial below beside each day. Then please return this sheet on Friday with your child. Thank you!

Monday _____   Wednesday _____

Tuesday _____   Thursday _____

Scented Soap Spelling

Pour a small amount of scented, liquid soap on a plate. Have your child spell her words into the soap using a different finger for each word.

Pantomimes

As you pantomime a spelling word, your child guesses the word and spells it. Then it will be your child's turn to pantomime a word and allow you to guess and spell.

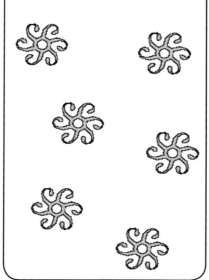

String Measuring

Have your child write her words on paper. Then give her a piece of string that you have cut to be exactly two inches long. Ask her to estimate if each of the words she wrote is shorter than or longer than two inches.

Parents,

Please spend five to ten minutes each day with your child helping him / her study their words and initial below beside each day. Then please return this sheet on Friday with your child. Thank you!

Monday _____   Wednesday _____
Tuesday _____   Thursday _____

Windex®Spelling

Spray something glass with Windex® Using a paper towel, ask your child to "clean" the glass by spelling each word into the Windex® and wiping it clean.

Silly Sentences

Think of a word that begins with each of the letters in the spelling word and construct a silly sentence. For instance, the word *does* might turn into: "David often eats snails." This is always more effective when it is paired with a picture or acted out.

And remember, the sillier the sentence, the better!

Parents,

Please spend five to ten minutes each day with your child helping him / her study their words and initial below beside each day. Then please return this sheet on Friday with your child. Thank you!

Monday _____   Wednesday _____
Tuesday _____   Thursday _____

Sew the Spelling Word

Write each of your child's words on a recipe card and punch holes in the card to outline the word. Using a large plastic needle and yarn, have your child sew the letters to complete the spelling of each word.

"Pat and Rub" Spelling

Have your child try rubbing her tummy while patting her head and at the same time spelling each of her words!

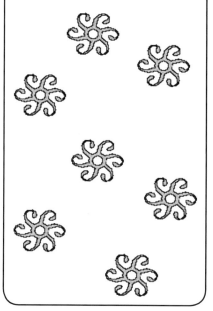

Finger Spelling

Have your child finger spell her spelling words for the week using the manual alphabet (see addendum).

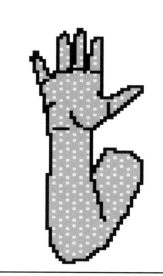

Parents,

Please spend five to ten minutes each day with your child helping him / her study their words and initial below beside each day. Then please return this sheet on Friday with your child. Thank you!

Monday _____   Wednesday _____
Tuesday _____   Thursday _____

The Alphabet
American Sign Language

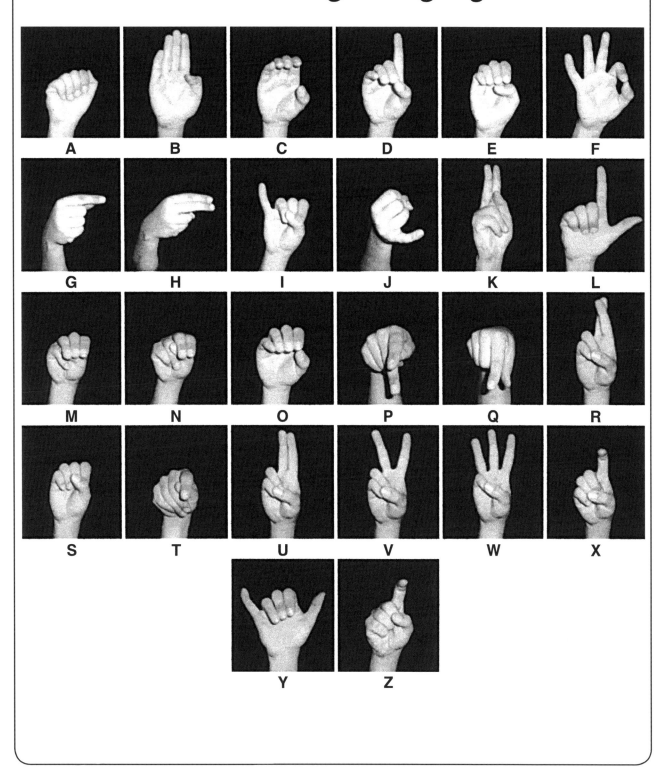

Bibliography

Bear, D., Invernizzi, M., Templeton, S., & Johnston, F. (2000). *Words Their Way: Word Study for Phonics, Vocabulary, and Spelling Instruction. Upper* Saddle River, NJ: Prentice Hall.

Bear, D., Templeton, S., & Warner, M. (1991). The development of a qualitative inventory of higher levels of orthographic knowledge. In J. Zutell & S. McCormick (Eds.), *Learner factors/teacher factors: Issues in literacy research and instruction: Fortieth yearbook of the National Reading Conference* (pp. 105-110). Chicago: NRC.

Bear, D. R., & Templeton, S. (1998). "Explorations in developmental spelling: Foundations for learning and teaching phonics, spelling, and vocabulary." *The Reading Teacher,* 52, 222-242.

Carnine, L., Carnine, D., & Gersten, R. (1984). "Analysis of oral reading errors made by economically disadvantaged students taught with a synthetic phonics approach." *Reading Research Quarterly, 19,* 343-356.

Clymer, T. (1963/1996). "The utility of phonic generalizations in the primary grades." *The Reading Teacher, 16,* 252-258. (Reprinted in *The Reading Teacher, 50,* 182-187, 1996)

Ehri, L. C. (1993). "How English orthography influences phonological knowledge as children learn to read and spell." In R.J. Scales (ed.), *Literacy and language analysis* (pp.21-43). Hillsdale, NJ: Lawrence Erlbaum.

Ehri, L. C. (1997). "Learning to read and learning to spell are one and the same, almost." In C. C. Perfetti, L. Rieban, & M. Fayol (Eds.), *Learning to spell - Research, theory, and practice across languages* (pp.237-269). Mahwah, NJ: Lawrence Erlbaum.

Ganske, K. (2000). *Word Journeys: Assessment-Guided Phonics, Spelling, and Vocabulary Instruction.* New York: Guilford.

Morris, D. (1982). " 'Word Sort': A categorization strategy for improving word recognition ability." *Reading Psychology, 3,* 247-259.

Templeton, S., & Morris, D. (1999). "Questions teachers ask about spelling." *Reading Research Quarterly, 34,* 102-112.

Thompson, R. (1930). *The Effectiveness of Modern Spelling Instruction.* New York: Columbia University Teacher's College (Contributions to Education, No. 436).

About the Author

With over 16 years of nation-wide experience, Lynne Ecenbarger is a highly sought-after educational speaker, motivator, and teacher trainer. Lynne has presented for ASCD, as well as State and National Reading Association Conferences and continues to speak regularly at seminars across the country for Staff Development for Educators (SDE) and Staff Development Resources (SDR). She presents also for the Indiana Association for Learning Disabilities and the Northeast Indiana Literacy Council. Lynne has been a contributing writer to *Learning Magazine* and *The Connection*, as well as a published author. Her book *Method Mania: Activities to Teach Comprehension Skills and Strategies* continues to be a best-seller for elementary classroom teachers.

Printed in the United States
105239LV00001B